We Drive Car Transporters

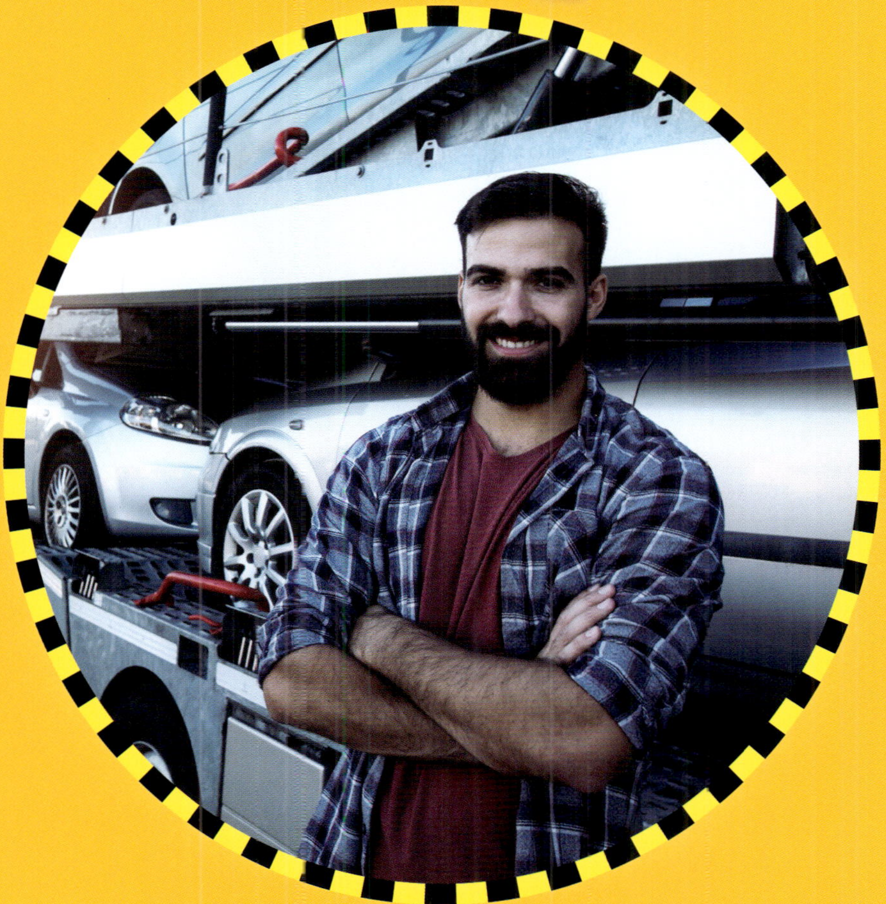

Alix Wood

Ruby Tuesday Books

Published in 2025 by Ruby Tuesday Books Ltd.

Copyright © 2025 Ruby Tuesday Books Ltd.

All rights reserved. No part of this publication may be reproduced in whole or in part, stored in any retrieval system, or transmitted in any form or by any means, electronic, mechanical, photocopying, recording, or otherwise, without written permission from the publisher.

Editors: Ruth Owen & Mark J. Sachner
Design & Production: Alix Wood

Photo credits:
Alamy: Cover (Taina Sohlman), 11T (Vitaliy Borushko), 11B (Justin Kase zninez), 12T (Manor Photography), 12B (Ronald Rampsch), 13T (Manor Photography), 17T (Malcolm Haines), 17B (Brett Keating), 20 (Stan Pritchard); Creative Commons: 10R; iStockPhoto: 16 (McCaig); Shutterstock: 1 (Aleksandar Malivuk), 3 (Krivosheev Vitaly), 4–5 (Felipe Sanchez), 5R (Standret/ESB Basic), 6T (Siwakorn1933), 6B (siriwat wongchana), 7T (Vitpho), 7B (Ronald Rampsch), 8T (Vitpho), 8B (Aerial-motion), 9T (Studio concept), 9B (boxthedog), 10L (Trygve Finkelsen), 13B (Iconic Bestiary), 15 (Bogdan Vacarciuc), 18T (Memory Stockphoto), 18B (Roman Babakin), 19T (CC7/Labrador Photo Video), 19B (Watch the World), 21T (woodsnorthphoto), 22 (Zentangle/Bjoern Wylezich/Ronald Rampsch), 23 (Magnifier/Wigphoto/Oleksiy Mark); Alix Wood: 14, 21B.

British Library Cataloguing in Publication Data (CIP) is available for this title.

ISBN 978-1-78856-585-1

Printed in Poland by L&C Printing Group

www.rubytuesdaybooks.com

Contents

What kind of truck delivers cars? 4

Glossary 22

Index 24

What kind of truck delivers cars?

Big trucks carry all kinds of things. Car transporters are trucks that deliver new cars.

New cars

Car transporter

Why should new cars ride on a truck instead of being driven to **car dealerships**?

A new car

Zero miles

Because no one wants a new car that has already driven hundreds of miles!

A car transporter driver starts their day early.

They check their truck is safe to drive.

The tyres will carry a lot of weight when the truck is full of heavy cars.

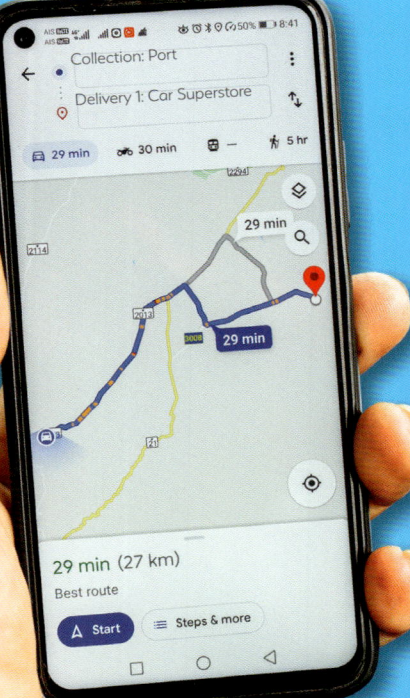

Drivers have to plan their **route** very carefully.

The transporter is too heavy and long for some roads.

The driver must check the load will fit under low bridges.

The driver fills the truck with fuel and sets off to pick up their load.

A driver may have a lot of cars to pick up, and a long way to drive.

A ship is unloading some brand new cars at a **port**.

Ship

New cars

8

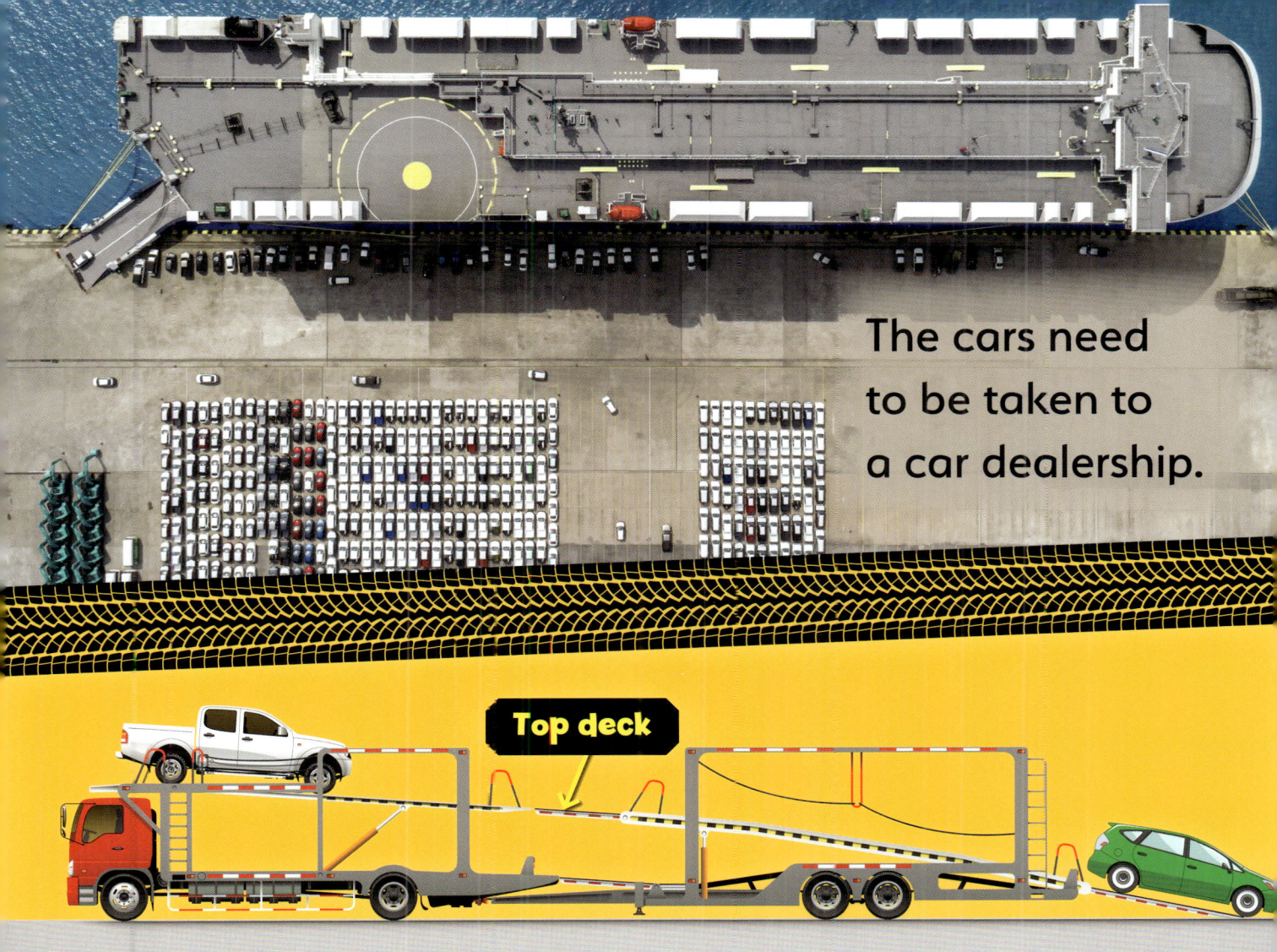

The cars need to be taken to a car dealership.

The car transporter arrives at the port. The driver lowers the truck's top **deck**.

The top deck is loaded first. Can you guess why?

To lower the top deck, the driver pushes a lever on the side of the truck.

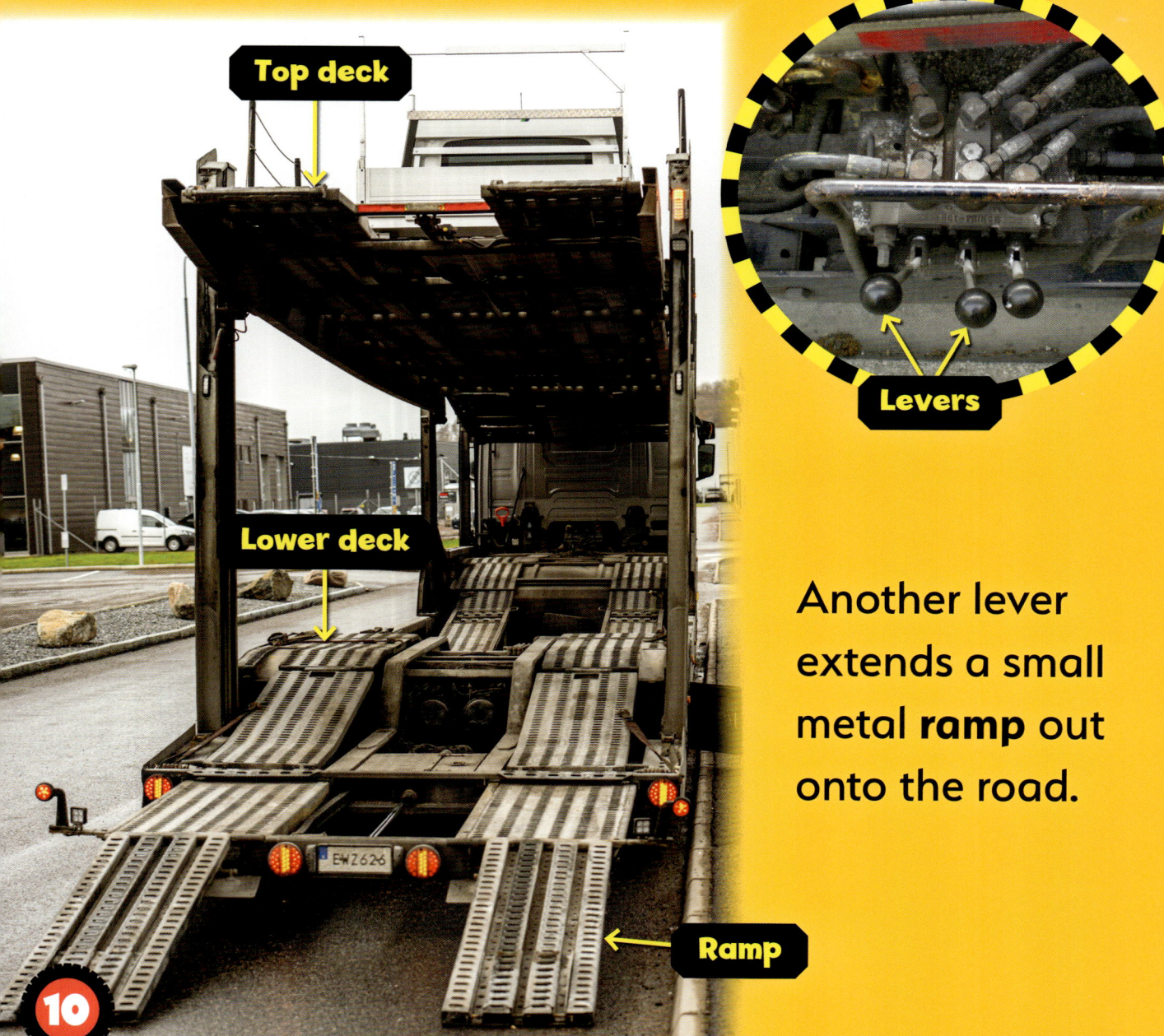

Top deck

Lower deck

Ramp

Levers

Another lever extends a small metal **ramp** out onto the road.

The driver starts the first car and drives it forwards or reverses it up the steep ramp.

The driver must stop quickly when the car reaches the end.

The driver gets out of the car very carefully – it's a long way down!

One by one, the driver fills the top deck with cars.

Chock

The driver ties the cars onto the truck with straps, chains and chocks.

Once a truck's top deck is full, the driver uses a lever to lift the deck up.

Top deck

Lower deck

Now the driver can load the lower deck.

If the lower deck was loaded first, the cars would be squashed when the driver lowered the top deck!

To check that each car will fit, the driver measures their height with a measuring stick.

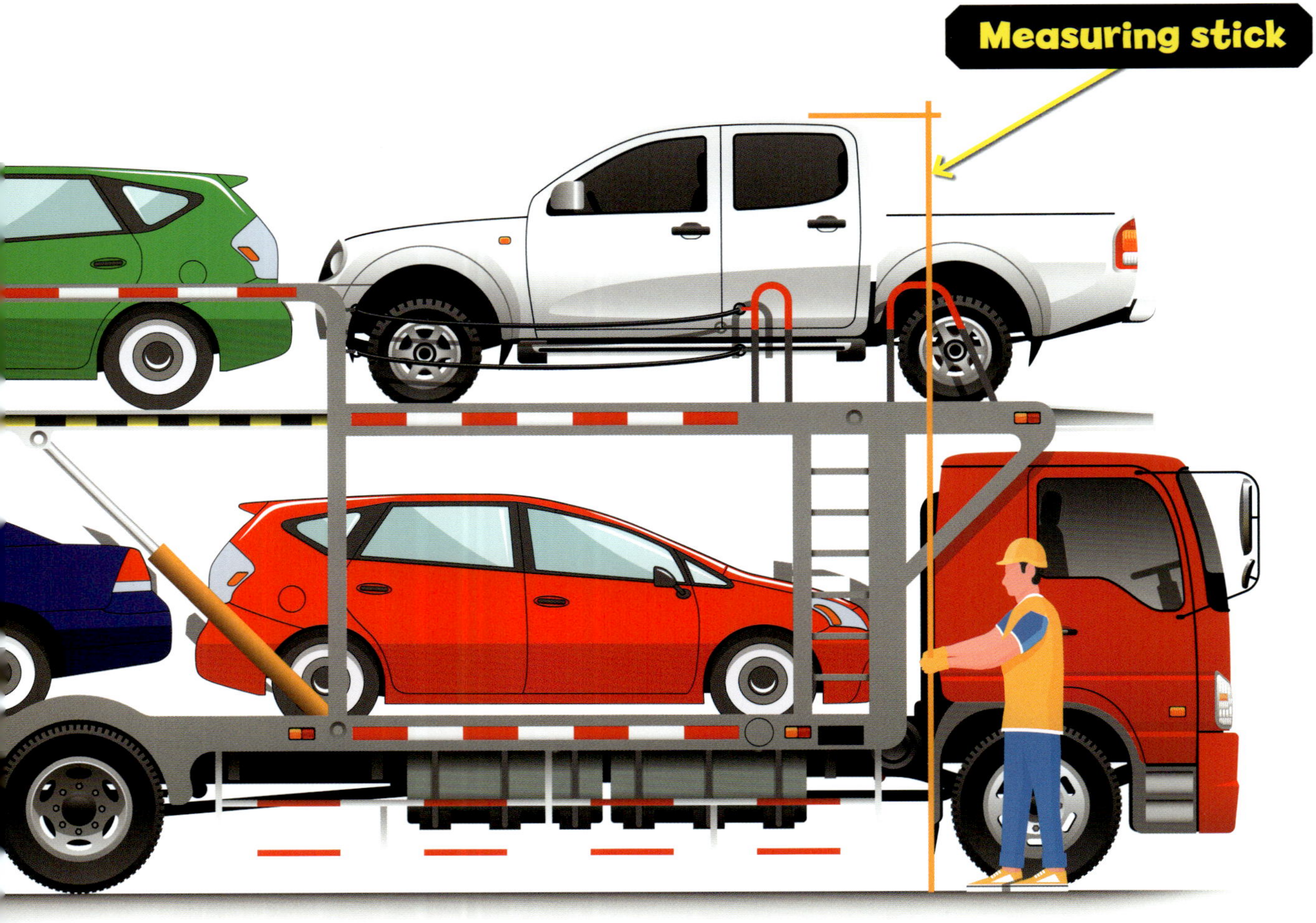

Measuring stick

The driver also measures the loaded truck's highest point with the stick.

The driver needs to know that the transporter will fit under any bridges on the route.

15

The new cars must be kept clean and scratch-free.

Sometimes they are covered with special plastic wrap.

The cars have gaps in the wrap, so the truck driver can open the doors and see to drive the cars on and off the transporter.

Plastic wrap

Gap

Closed car transporter

Classic car

Expensive racing cars and classic, or old, cars might be carried in a closed car transporter.

Closed car transporter

Racing car

Some cars may have been in an accident and are too damaged to drive.

Car transporters take these cars to be repaired or to a scrapyard.

A damaged car is loaded onto a car transporter with a winch.

Steel rope

Winch

Hook

The car is hooked onto the winch.

The truck's driver presses a button, and the winch pulls the car onto the transporter.

At a scrapyard, the metal from damaged cars is recycled and helps make new cars.

A full car transporter is slow and heavy, and the cars creak and groan.

Car transporter drivers don't worry.

They know the cars are strapped on tight!

When a car transporter arrives at a dealership, the driver unloads the cars.

Car dealership

The lower deck is unloaded first.

Then the top deck is unloaded.

Then, the driver parks their transporter. Tomorrow will be another busy day delivering cars.

Glossary

car dealership
A business where people can buy new cars.

chock
An object that is used to stop a wheel moving on a vehicle or plane.

deck
A floor or one layer of a truck or a ship.

port
A large harbour on the coast where ships come to load and unload goods.

ramp
A sloping surface that joins two different levels of floor or ground.

route
The roads taken to get from one place to another.

Index

C
car dealerships 5, 9, 21
cars 4–5, 8–9
classic cars 17
closed car transporters 17

D
damaged cars 18–19
decks 9, 10, 12–13, 21

L
loading and unloading cars
    8–9, 10–11, 12–13, 19, 21

M
measuring 14–15

P
ports 8–9

R
racing cars 17
ramps 10–11
route planning 6–7, 15

S
scrapyards 18–19

T
tyres 6